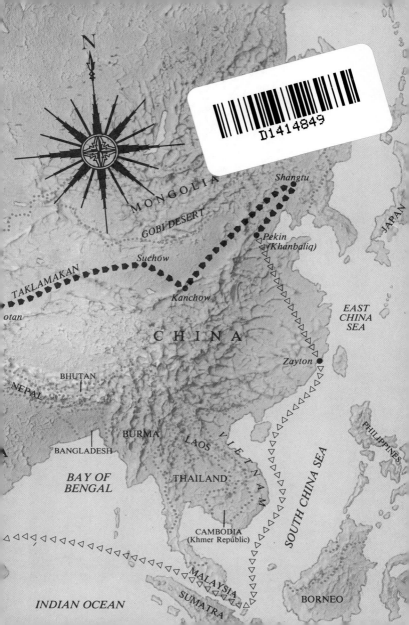

Marco Polo was one of the greatest travellers of all time, and almost the first man from Europe to see the wonderful world of East Asia. When he returned to Venice, he wrote the story of his travels. He told of giraffes and crocodiles, of the first printed money and of the magnificence of the Great Khan. Here are some of his tales.

Acknowledgment
Some of the source material for this book was taken from the original title *Marco Polo* by L. du Garde Peach.
The front endpaper map is by Gerald Witcomb.

Marco Polo

by AUDREY DALY
with illustrations by ROGER HALL

Ladybird Books Loughborough

Marco Polo was born in Venice in the year 1254. Venice was a city of great wealth, power and splendour, and a wonderful place to live in. It was built on a number of little islands, which meant that it didn't have streets like an ordinary city, it had canals. When people went to visit their friends, they often had to go by boat.

Venice was important because it was at the centre of a great network of sea routes, and Venetian merchants traded with the farthest limits of the known world. They bought luxuries such as silks, spices, carpets and precious stones from the east, and they

sent fleets loaded with these and other luxuries to trading fairs held as far away as Stourbridge on the River Ouse, in England. Every great port had quays which belonged to the Venetians.

Seven hundred years ago, travelling about the world was very much more dangerous and difficult than it is today. Indeed, many people still thought the Earth was flat. Europeans knew little or nothing about those who lived on the other side of the world, even though they bought and used the goods that came from those distant lands.

5

The main reason for the lack of knowledge was the enormous distances the information had to travel. Merchants had to work in relays: one group would meet another and hand on its goods. The Silk Road, as the trading route across Asia to the capital of China was called, was seven thousand miles (11,265 kilometres) long. So in the course of a journey, goods changed hands many times. The sailors who brought them the last short stage of the journey could tell

nothing of the lands from which the silks and jewels had originally come.

Since the profits were very great on luxuries like silk and spices, some merchants were willing to undertake long and difficult journeys to obtain them. Marco Polo was the son of just such an adventurous merchant, Nicolo Polo. When Marco was fifteen, his father and his uncle, Maffeo, returned from a trading journey which had lasted many years.

They had been all the way to the capital of China, Pekin, and had been kindly received there by the Mongol Emperor, Kubla Khan, sometimes called the Great Khan. He had been interested in all they told him about the way people lived in the western world.

The idea of the Christian religion had interested the Great Khan most of all. He had asked the two Venetians to go back to Italy with a letter from him to the Pope. In it, he asked the Pope to send him some Christian monks. He had also asked the Polo brothers to return to his court with the monks.

He had asked them too to bring some of the oil from the famous lamp in the Church of the Holy Sepulchre at Jerusalem. This lamp was supposed to have been burning for a thousand years without going out.

When Nicolo and Maffeo Polo at last arrived back in Venice, however, they found that the old Pope had died. The Khan's request would have to wait until a new Pope had been chosen.

Two years passed and still there was no new Pope. Tired of waiting, the Polo brothers made up their minds to set out once more on the long and dangerous journey to Pekin. Marco was now seventeen, and they decided to take him with them.

It was in the year 1271 that Marco Polo went aboard a little ship in the harbour at Venice, with his father and uncle. His journey was to last three and a half years, and would make him one of the most famous travellers of all time.

From Venice they sailed down the Adriatic Sea then through the Mediterranean to the port of Acre, which was near Jerusalem in Palestine. Here they met a priest called Theobald.

Nicolo and Maffeo had met Theobald on their way home to Venice, when he had told them that nothing could be done about the Khan's requests until a new Pope was elected. At this second meeting with him they talked about the problem once more, but Theobald could not give them any more help than before.

Since they were quite near Jerusalem, at least one request could be fulfilled — the oil from the Holy Lamp. They went to collect this, then returned to Acre to find that there was still no news of a new Pope. Theobald did however give them a letter to Kubla Khan testifying that they had done all they could to fulfil the Khan's wishes.

Now Nicolo, Maffeo and Marco left Acre for Ayas, which was the city from which merchants travelling to the east usually started.

When they arrived at Ayas, it seemed as if their luck had suddenly changed for the better. A message awaited them from Theobald — he was now Gregory X, the new Pope! They were summoned to his presence, so that he could help them.

When they met him again, Pope Gregory sent a personal message to Kubla Khan, and many costly gifts. He also provided two Dominican friars to go to the Great Khan's court.

The Polos set out once more, this time with the full blessing of the Pope and with the Christian monks the Khan had requested.

When the little party of five reached Ayas however,

trouble began again. From Ayas the road lay eastwards through Armenia. It was a rough and difficult road, sometimes becoming a mere track across desert sands, and very hard to follow. Rivers had to be forded, and often the way led along narrow ledges cut in the side of steep cliffs. Far below, in deep rocky gorges, were dangerous rapids.

The two friars were men with little spirit of adventure, and the thought of this road filled them with fear. When in addition they met a party of armed men who told them that there was fighting going on in Armenia, it was too much for them. They refused to go any further, and turned back, leaving the Pope's gifts to the Great Khan with the Polos.

So the three Venetians set off alone. They travelled sometimes on foot, sometimes on mules or camels, and camped at night under the stars. Marco must have felt a long way from his comfortable home in Venice.

They took a northerly route, to avoid the fighting. Marco was now in country such as he had never seen before, and he took careful note of everything he saw on the way.

One of the strange sights which he remembered was a fountain of oil which came up out of the earth. The people who lived nearby told him that it never stopped, day or night. Marco's notes tell us, 'This oil is not good to eat, but it is good for burning, and as a salve for men or camels afflicted with itch or scab. Men come from a long distance to fetch this oil.'

This place is known to the modern world as the Baku oilfield, which supplies vast quantities of oil for petrol for today's aeroplanes and cars.

Marco also listened to many stories and local legends, which he afterwards wrote down. One of these was about Noah's Ark which, he was told, was still to be seen on top of a high mountain, Mount Ararat, where it had landed after the Flood.

The three travellers now turned south, making for the Persian Gulf, where they hoped to find a ship to take them round India, on the way to China. If they could go by sea, they would not have to cross the dangerous Gobi desert.

Now they were travelling only about twenty miles (32 kilometres) a day, because the road was very bad. The weather was very hot too, which meant that they had to rest for three or four hours in the middle of each day.

During this part of their long journey, they visited the famous city of Baghdad, which Marco described as 'the noblest and most extensive city to be found in

this part of the world.' It was a splendid city, with brightly tiled mosques and minarets, surrounded by groves of palm trees and beautiful gardens.

Baghdad was noted for velvet and cloth of gold and rich brocades, which no doubt interested the merchants from Venice. It was also the city of Harun-al-Raschid and the *Arabian Nights Entertainment*, those wonderful stories from which come the well known *Ali Baba and the Forty Thieves,* and *Aladdin and his Wonderful Lamp.*

Baghdad was most famous however as a centre for learning. Astronomy and science were among the subjects which were studied there.

The town towards which Marco and his father and uncle were going was called Kerman. The journey had now become a very pleasant one. They had been travelling with a number of other merchants, together with their slaves and guards. In this part of the world, where robbers and bandits were often met, this was safer than travelling alone.

The road was not always through deserts or over high, dangerous passes. There were regions of rich country pastures, and even in the deserts there were oases of palm trees. Marco told of hunting and hawking as the days went by.

He also told of a local legend connected with the three Wise Men who visited the baby Jesus at Bethlehem. The three Wise Men were buried in very beautiful tombs at a town called Saveh, which Marco visited on his journey. The legend said that the Christ child's parting gift to the Wise Men was a small casket. When they opened it, all it contained was a small stone, which they threw down a well in disappointment. The well burst into miraculous flame, and had been burning ever since.

At Kerman the road forked. Travellers to the east either took the northern route, to the north of Afghanistan, or turned south to Hormuz, a port at the end of the Persian Gulf.

The southern road, which Marco now travelled, was through very wild and mountainous country. Sometimes, on a high mountain pass, he suffered

from the intense cold, only to descend to a plain where the heat was stifling.

It was on this road that the party of merchants was attacked by bandits called the Karaunas, who terrorised the region. They were believed to raise a 'magic fog' when they attacked, to confuse and frighten their victims. Nowadays we think this was a 'dry fog,' caused by fine dust particles stirred up by the hot winds, but this had not been explained in Marco Polo's time.

There was a battle between the bandits and the men guarding the caravan of merchants. There were not many guards however and things went badly for them.

The Polos fled to the safety of a nearby walled town called Kamasal, and their baffled attackers rode off.

A few days later the Polos reached Hormuz without further danger. Marco, with his father and uncle, went to the quay to look for a ship.

They could not find one suitable for the long voyage round the south of India. The Polos could hardly believe that sailors would trust their lives to some of the ships in Hormuz harbour. Marco said they 'were of the worst kind, and dangerous for navigation'. The planks were fastened with wooden pegs instead of nails, and bound together with ropes made of the husks of coconuts. Even today, in the Persian Gulf, you may see boats made in this fashion.

These ships had only one sail and no anchor, and in bad weather they were often driven ashore and wrecked.

Nicolo decided that rather than take the risk of sailing in such a ship, it would be safer to return to Kerman and take the overland road to China.

Marco was glad to leave Hormuz, which he had found uncomfortably hot and very depressing. When anyone died there, the women had to mourn for four years, lamenting and wailing at least once a day.

It was with mixed feelings that they set out on the two hundred mile (322 kilometre) journey back to Kerman. They remembered the cold of the mountain passes and the heat of the plains. Most of all, they remembered the bandits.

They travelled cautiously, and managed to reach Kerman safely. From here they again set off eastwards.

The country which they now had to cross was naked desert. There was nothing but sand, neither trees nor water, and the heat was intense. Even wild animals avoided it.

They spent many days crossing this desert, coming at last to the town of Balkh.

Here, they were told, Alexander the Great was married to Princess Roxana, daughter of the King of Persia. Marco noted that 'the palaces of Balkh are all in ruins'.

Here again the road divided. One way went north to Samarkand, another south via Kabul and Peshawar, and a third north-west through Bokhara.

After talking with camel-drivers, however, Nicolo decided to travel due east to Kashgar.

Although this way was shorter, it meant that they would have to cross some high and very mountainous country, known as the 'Roof of the World'. This was the Plain of Pamir, 15,600 feet (4,755 metres) above sea level, through which the River Oxus flows to the Aral Sea.

Marco noted how hard it was to climb to this high tableland, for it was more difficult country than any across which they had so far travelled.

There were a number of things which surprised them. There were no birds and no people living there at all. It was also intensely cold. When they came to cook their food, they found that, in Marco's words, 'however extraordinary it may be thought, from the

keenness of the air, fires when lighted do not give the same heat as in lower situations, nor produce the same effect in dressing victuals.'

Marco thought the intense cold caused it, but we know today that there is less oxygen in the air at high altitudes. This means that water boils at a lower temperature and therefore food takes longer to cook.

Marco described a wild sheep with large curling horns that lives on the Plains of Pamir. It was named after him — *Ovis Poli* — although he was not the first person to describe it.

Marco, Maffeo and Nicolo left the Plain of Pamir and crossed the northern end of Kashmir, one of the most beautiful countries in the world. They passed through Kashgar, which Marco noted had beautiful gardens and vineyards, and through Khotan, famous for its jade mines. (Jade is a very hard precious stone, which is usually a pale green but is sometimes cream or white. It is often used for carved ornaments as well as jewellery.)

Then the scene changed for they had come to the worst of all the deserts they had had to face. Although this desert is sometimes called the Gobi desert, this name really belongs to the large desert of Mongolia, north-east of Marco's route. The name of the frightening place that the Polos came to after leaving Kashgar is Taklamakan. It was to take them more than a month to cross, and the water-holes lay more than a day's march apart.

It was a grim and forbidding place, with no life at all except for an occasional oasis. Marco says of it: 'It is a well known fact that this desert is the abode of evil spirits, which lure travellers to their destruction. Losing the right path, and not knowing how to get back to it, they perish miserably of hunger.'

Marco also saw the strange *mirage* of the desert. In a mirage, lakes and trees and even buildings seem to appear in the midst of the sands. This is because the light from real buildings, trees and other objects (which are much further on and below the horizon) has been mirrored by a layer of hot air.

After they had thankfully left the desert behind, the Polos came to Suchow, in Tangut province. They were delighted to see green fields and fertile valleys, and to be amongst people once more. They stayed in this region for some time. Marco mentioned *asbestos* in his notes and how fireproof cloth was made from it, for it was mined in this area.

Then the Polos moved on to Kanchow, where they made another long stay. Here Marco must have seen the Great Wall of China for the first time.

This wall is one of the wonders of the world. It was built more than two thousand years ago and its purpose was to keep the northern barbarians out of China.

It still stands today, 1,400 miles (2,250 kilometres) long, through valleys and over mountains. Originally it was twenty feet (6 metres) high, and so thick that two carriages could drive side by side along the top of it. At short intervals there were strong towers from which soldiers guarded the frontier.

It is strange that Marco Polo, who mentioned so many things, said nothing about the Great Wall.

When the travellers moved on once more, they turned north-east, because they had learnt that the Khan was at his northern capital of Shangtu. While they were still forty days' journey away from their journey's end, the Polos were met by messengers from Kubla Khan.

There were of course no telephones in those days, but the Chinese had a system of carrying messages which was very well planned and remarkably fast.

Broad post roads led from the capital to all the provinces, with post houses about twenty miles (32 kilometres) apart. Men and horses were always on duty, and when an important letter had to be carried a great distance, it was carried from one post house to the next, day and night, like a relay race. Fresh horses

were kept harnessed, ready to set off as soon as a rider arrived.

In this way a message could be carried well over two hundred miles (322 kilometres) in a day. The postmen did not only carry messages: sometimes they brought rare fruits to the capital for the Great Khan's table, freshly picked in a distant province.

By means of this postal system, the Great Khan had heard of the approach of the Venetians, even though they were still so far away from his Palace.

The next forty days were, however, very different from the hard grim weeks in the desert. The travellers were now under Kubla Khan's protection, honoured guests to be received everywhere with respect and afforded every comfort and protection.

When at last they arrived at Shangtu, the Khan's Summer Palace must have been a wonderful sight. It was built of white marble, and the halls and rooms

were decorated with gold. Now Marco Polo met the Great Khan for the first time, and found him magnificent but surprisingly human.

He noted, 'He is a man of good stature, neither tall nor short, but of moderate height. His complexion is fair and ruddy like a rose, the eyes black and handsome, the nose shapely and set squarely in place.'

The Khan was very pleased with the letter and presents from the Pope, and made the Polos welcome, with great honour.

The journey from Venice to China had taken more than three years. From time to time, Nicolo and Maffeo Polo and young Marco with them had remained for weeks or months in towns where they had been able to carry on their business as merchants.

Marco was a young man of twenty, and was delighted to have arrived safely at the Khan's court. Perhaps he might not have been quite so delighted had he known he was going to stay there for the next seventeen years!

He remained for some months at the Summer Palace, and took part in the hunting expeditions which were the Khan's favourite amusement.

He wrote about many things which he saw at the Court. There was the Khan's 'portable palace', which he used as the centre for his summer hunting. It was made of bamboo cane, held in position by silken ropes. Like a tent, it could be taken down and moved to the next place the Khan wished to go to.

Marco was also interested in the Great Khan's magicians, who were from Tibet and Kashmir. They could make the Khan's drinking cups float through the air to his hand while everyone watched, and they were supposed to be able to ensure good weather for his hunting.

The capital of China was Khanbaliq, which stood where Pekin stands today. After a summer of hunting, the Khan and his court moved back to the capital, taking Marco with them.

He wrote a great deal about Khanbaliq, for he found it very impressive. It was a wonderful city, with beautiful straight roads meeting at right angles and enclosed by a rectangular wall. It was surrounded by a high wall, with twelve gates and many towers, and each gate was guarded by a thousand soldiers.

In the centre of the city there was a great bell which was tolled every night. After the third stroke of the bell, no one was allowed to go about the streets, except on urgent business.

Kubla Khan's palace stood high on a marble platform, and had a brightly coloured roof, with tiles of red, green, blue and yellow. Inside, the walls were decorated in gold and covered with pictures. In the great banqueting hall, said Marco, six thousand guests could be served at one time.

Marco Polo was soon high in favour with Kubla Khan, who quickly realised that he was honest and trustworthy.

He was also diligent and hard-working, and set himself to learn the four principal languages of China. As a result, he was employed by the Khan on affairs of state. He spent three years at Hangchow, for example, on important work in the Khan's diplomatic service.

Marco was interested in everything he saw, and wrote it down. Among many other things, he told of the printed paper money, made from the bark of mulberry trees, which the Chinese were using hundreds of years before it was introduced into Western Europe. These paper notes were stamped with the royal seal in red ink, and could be used anywhere in the Chinese Empire.

Strangely enough, he did not mention the printing of books, which the Chinese had invented some time before.

By now, Marco Polo was so trusted by the Khan that he was sent on important business to parts of China many hundreds of miles (kilometres) from Khanbaliq (Pekin).

He travelled as far as Malaya, Sumatra and Ceylon, which we believe he saw at least three times on various journeys. He mentioned the sapphires of Ceylon, which are famous to this day.

When Marco wrote his famous book *A Description of the World* many years later, he tried to give a picture of the countries through which he travelled.

Some of the places and things he mentioned he probably knew only by hearsay, from other people. This could account for some of the 'tall stories' he told which many people just didn't believe.

He was called 'Il Milione' by the Venetians, because he exaggerated so much. He often referred to 'great numbers' of white horses, 'great wealth', and

'the costliest stones'. According to him, too, Tibet had 'the greatest rogues and the greatest robbers in the world'.

Nor did they always believe his descriptions of strange animals. Certainly the 'gryphon bird', which ate elephants, is a work of imagination. The modern world however is quite familiar with giraffes and crocodiles, both of which he saw and described.

Mining sapphires

One of his journeys took him to Karaian, the country today known as Burma. He was three and a half months on the way, travelling in great state, with soldiers and servants, as the Khan's representative. He visited places with wonderful names such as Karazan, Kain-du, and Yachi, the chief town of Karaian.

At a place called Mien, he saw a wonderful tomb, consisting of two pyramids. One pyramid was covered with silver and the other with gold, an inch (25 millimetres) in thickness. On top of each was a golden ball, surrounded by little bells, which rang every time the wind blew.

On other journeys he travelled far to the north, where he saw snow and ice, and people dressed in skins, travelling on sledges.

He heard of cannibals on yet another journey, and described them as 'nasty brutish folk who kill men for food'. He told of a tree that dripped wine (the *toddy-palm*), and of flour which came from a tree — this was what we now call sago.

After seventeen years in China, Marco Polo had become a rich man, and he began to think of returning to Venice. Kubla Khan was growing old, and Marco was afraid of what might happen to him if the Great Khan was to die.

Nicolo and Maffeo were also growing old. They too had become successful in China, and now wished to spend the rest of their lives in their own country.

Kubla Khan was reluctant to let them go. Marco Polo was not only his most trusted servant, the Khan was fond of him, too. Then it chanced that a Chinese princess was preparing to travel by sea to Hormuz, to marry the King of Persia.

The ambassadors who had come to conduct her asked that the three Venetians might go with them on the return voyage, because they were known to be clever at navigation.

Kubla Khan agreed, and a squadron of fourteen ships was fitted out. They sailed from China in the year 1292. Marco was now thirty eight years old. There were many delays, and the voyage to Persia lasted two years.

When at last Marco Polo reached Persia, he heard that Kubla Khan had died. The three Venetians had now no reason to return to China.

The young King of Persia gave them golden passports which meant that they would have horses, provisions and a guard to protect them throughout his dominions. Without these passports, they would have been in great danger of being killed on this last stage of their journey home.

It was in 1295 that they finally arrived back in Venice, twenty four years after they had left it.

They had been away so long that no one recognised them. They were dressed in the worn clothing in which they had been travelling, and they had almost forgotten how to speak Italian. Their stories of the wonders of Kubla Khan's palaces were disbelieved, and the merchants of Venice made fun of them.

The three travellers were not quite as poor as they looked, however. Ripping open the seams of their shabby coats, they produced handfuls of rich jewels.

How did Marco Polo's story come to be written?

Perhaps Marco had a wonderful memory or, more probably, he kept notes of all the places he visited, because he was able to dictate all the strange and unusual facts that are set down in his book, *A Description of the World*.

All we know for certain is that it was written down by a man called Rusticello who was a prisoner in Genoa at the same time as Marco Polo. They had been captured by the Genoese in a sea fight between the galleys of Venice and Genoa. Marco Polo had commanded one of the Venetian galleys.

He returned to Venice for the second time in 1299, his adventures over at last. He settled down and had

three daughters. We know from his will that he was not rich when he died in 1324, so the great wealth his travels had brought him had not lasted.

His book, however, with its wonderful picture of the teeming life of the East, has given him a place in history. His name will always be remembered as one of the most remarkable travellers of all time.

INDEX